GOVERNMENT'S PLACE IN THE MARKET

GOVERNMENT'S PLACE IN THE MARKET

Eliot Spitzer

A Boston Review Book

THE MIT PRESS Cambridge, Mass. London, England

MIT Press books may be purchased at special quantity discounts for business or sales promotional use. For information, please e-mail special_sales@mitpress.mit.edu or write to Special Sales Department, The MIT Press, 55 Hayward Street, Cambridge, MA 02142.

This book was set in Adobe Garamond by *Boston Review* and was printed and bound in the United States of America.

Library of Congress Cataloging-in-Publication Data
Spitzer, Eliot
  Government's place in the market / Eliot Spitzer.
     p. cm.
  "A Boston Review Book."
  ISBN 978-0-262-01570-7 (hbk. : alk. paper)
  1. Trade regulation—United States. 2. Markets—Law and legislation—United States. 3. Corporate governance—Government policy—United States. I. Title.
  HD3616.U47S65   2011
  381'.30973—dc22
                                          2010051898

10   9   8   7   6   5   4   3   2   1

To Silda, Elyssa, Sarabeth, and Jenna,
with much love

CONTENTS

Introduction 1

I Government's Place in the Market 13

II Forum

Dean Baker 59

Robert Johnson 67

III Common Sense 77

ABOUT THE CONTRIBUTORS 85

Introduction

How quickly the moment passes! Merely two years after the worst economic crisis in nearly a century, we have forgotten what little we learned and have lapsed back into the rhetoric and behavior that caused the crisis in the first place.

Let's recap for a moment: in the immediate aftermath of the bankruptcy of the entire financial system, there was a consensus that the libertarianism that had dominated Washington for 30 years was an abject failure. The repeal of critical statutes that had structured the financial-services industry for decades and the lax enforcement of those few rules that remained simply did not work. Not only did we bring ourselves to financial ruin, but even the prior era of supposed "prosperity," we now saw, was characterized by declining middle-class incomes, increasing income inequality, and a hollowing-out of the areas of the economy that actually produced goods. Investment-banking profits alone could not sustain an economy. Excess leverage and debt drove wonderful returns for those few at the top who could manipulate capital and extract short-term profits, but it did not lead to sustainable economic growth. To the extent that we had an industrial policy during this era, most came to acknowledge that it was geared toward buttressing finance over real production, and the consequence was that vast sectors of our economy were unable to compete with newly invigorated nations around the world.

In the brief moment during which the post-crisis consensus held, the nature of public-policy debate was altered. Meaningful conversations produced eclectic and important thoughts on a new financial-regulatory regime and the response to U.S. competitive disadvantages in education, energy, and infrastructure investment. Americans began to discuss the necessary relationship between government and the market. Neither rigid libertarianism nor anti-market naiveté—the claim that competition and markets cannot work—were any longer credible. What emerged from these conversations was a more nuanced understanding of government's role in insuring the underpinnings of a real marketplace: competition, transparency, and integrity, and social investments that are not satisfied when left exclusively to the private sector. Fleshing out the rules of this understanding, and appreciating that this balanced approach was what had worked during the periods of our nation's great prosperity, was the task at hand. It was critical that this discussion rise above the pure rhetoric and political demagoguery that could so easily distract voters and lawmakers from the more subtle ideas at play.

But then the reality of politics emerged. The Obama administration failed to hold together a reform coalition in the face of an unrelenting assault from the right. The banks and others who had been bailed out early pushed back aggressively against any continued discussion about the proper role of government, apparently reasoning that once they had received what they needed, the door to further public spending should be closed. And just as significantly, the Obama administration was captured by a status quo alignment led by economic advisor Larry Summers and Treasury Secretary Timothy Geithner: once the banks were restored to solvency, only the most limited reforms to the structural failings that led to the cataclysm would be implemented. Those who sought either a significant ideological shift or a political leadership that would hold Wall Street accountable in even the slightest manner felt abandoned.

The Tea Party was left to fill the breach. It played to the anger and frustration that the Obama administration should have captured in support of genuine reform. Instead we got the wild success of the Tea Party, and possible reversion to pre-crisis policies.

At the moment when he could have created an alliance behind thoughtful principles that would mediate between the government and the private sector, President Obama punted entirely. He failed to create an intellectual or political argument for government intervention in the market. Hence he became susceptible to the attack that he simply sought a growing carnivorous government that would consume all that lay in front of it. He failed to make a case either for the interventions and rules that mattered, or against the ones that didn't. The failure to articulate boundaries lent credibility (in the eyes of some) to Tea Party and Republican claims that the Obama agenda was to socialize the economy. Nobody heard a persuasive or even coherent argument to the contrary. With the auto manufacturers, health providers, big pharma, and Wall Street all apparently eating out of the public trough while the middle class received nothing meaningful, is it any surprise that a backlash erupted?

So where does this leave us? The newly empowered Republican Party—the "Party of No," but now amped up—wants to repeal the health-care bill and pull back even the limited new rules put in place in the Dodd-Frank Wall Street Reform and Consumer Protection Act. The first new rule they will attack—the Volcker rule, which bars certain banks from making proprietary trades—is arguably the most important. Most perverse of all, even though the public grasps that Wall Street really was at the root of the problem, the Wall Street firms are once again positioned to dictate policy to a largely Republican Congress. Influential financiers and willing legislators are reestablishing the pernicious falsehood that regulation, rather than Wall Street greed, is responsible for our dire situation.

And who is going to win from all this at the end of the day? Unfortunately, as the U.S. economy continues to sputter, the long-term trend lines that really matter go unattended. We have solved the momentary financial crisis by having the public assume the enormous debts of the over-leveraged banks and restoring the banks' solvency, yet we have failed to address the structural issues that lead to declining middle-class income and national competitiveness.

How quickly we forget; how quickly we return to the ways that brought us to the precipice in the first place. And with the additional, enormous debt overhang of multiple bailouts now weighing us down, it gets harder and harder to see how there is a happy ending to this story. China, India, Brazil, even Russia, are smiling at our inability to be wiser when it really matters.

That is why now, more than ever, we cannot allow ourselves to be demoralized by events. We must have the serious conversation about government's proper role in the market that never emerged from its infancy. In these pages, I aim to show what that role looks like and why it is so critical to a stable and prosperous American future.

I

*Government's Place
in the Market*

EVERY DAY WE READ THE HEADLINES, feel the tensions, observe the consequences of the recent failures of market and government. Having a serious conversation about how to remedy these failures lies at the heart of current American politics. And that conversation should address three distinct questions:

- What are the parameters of government intervention in the marketplace? What rules should we use in deciding when the government should act and when it should let the market take its course?

- Has our response to the immediate crisis been successful?
- How might we restore an effective structure for corporate governance, the failures of which account for much of our economic troubles over the past 30 years?

Answers to the first question, about government intervention, have changed quickly. Ayn Rand was an articulate, powerful voice for libertarianism, the notion that each of us individually deserves to own what he or she creates, and that the role of government must be minimized. For 30 years a libertarian ideology dominated leadership circles, beginning politically with President Ronald Reagan, who led a fundamental transformation in our civic discourse about the government's role in everything from marginal tax rates to regulation. Many people think that Reagan was brilliant, and that his policies were necessary. Whether or not you agree with that assessment, you have to acknowledge that the Reagan agenda was ascendant until the fall of 2008, when the entire economic world appeared to collapse.

A year later we had Ken Feinberg, appointed by President Obama to determine how much CEOs would be paid. We went from abhorring government intervention to accepting a bureaucrat's decision on an executive's stock options. Today the antipathy toward Wall Street that peaked with the bailouts and enabled the creation of Feinberg's position—"Pay Czar"—is about all that unites liberals with the Republican right. But angry populism—180 degrees from libertarianism—is no better a guide than Rand. We understand the public anger, we sympathize with it, we all feel it. When the very people responsible for the cataclysm are reaping its rewards, we know something is wrong. But angry populism doesn't direct action. We are still left to figure out what government should do.

Liberal cynicism and conservative cries of "socialism" have occluded that process. Even now, two and a half years since the collapse, we haven't talked about the new rules we need, rules that dictate when government should intervene, where, why, and with what limits. I will articulate three such rules (and one footnote) in this effort.

Rule 1. Only government can ensure integrity, transparency, and fair dealing.

When I was Attorney General of New York, we investigated what I refer to as the "analyst cases." The cases were about investment banking. To understand them, all you need to know about investment banking is that the business has two sides: you have supposed analysts, who recommend stocks for investors to buy, and you have underwriters, who sell initial public offerings, secondary offerings, and other financial products that raise capital for the companies. But these two sides are often under the same roof. We argued that there is an inherent conflict of interest when the people who recommend a stock to retail investors—who say, "this is a great stock, buy it"—are also doing the underwriting. The more successful the underwriting, the more fees it will generate, and the more favorable the analysis, the more likely the underwriting will succeed.

This is clearly a conflict of interest. In fact, Jack Grubman, the telecom analyst banned from the securities industry in 2002, brilliantly encapsulated this whole era: what used to be viewed as a conflict of interest, he said, is now viewed as a "synergy." Think about that. What once was seen as dangerous to people, something to warn them about, is turned into something that creates value. This was the way we masked the problem. In the analyst cases, we didn't discover the conflict of interest—everyone understood it and had accepted it for a long time. But at the attorney general's office, we called it what it was.

We started with Merrill Lynch, but we went after all the big investment banks—what are called the "bulge bracket" firms. We found graphic emails. Analysts were saying, "this stock is a piece of ———," and at the same time telling people to buy it, buy it, buy it.

But things began to get really interesting after we had put our case together. We were about to file when I got a call from the lawyer for Merrill. He said to me, and this was arguably his most persuasive point, "Eliot, be careful, we have powerful friends." I said, "Okay, I'm not sure that's a legal argument." Actually, what I said to him I won't repeat verbatim. Needless to say, we went ahead.

The lawyers for Merrill came into my office. Now, when you're a white-collar defense lawyer, you argue in the alternative. First you say the emails were taken out of context. Then you say: "you don't fully understand them." Then you say, "no, they were fabricated." Then you say the emailer doesn't really speak on behalf of the company. And then you check the limits on your insurance. I was a white-collar defense attorney for a number of years, so I know the drill.

The Merrill lawyers didn't make any of those arguments. They came to me and said, in essence, "Eliot, you're right. Absolutely right about the conflicts, the tensions, the problems. But we are not as bad as our competitors." That was their defense to the charge that they were defrauding their customers and the marketplace. When I asked to hear more about it, they said, "let me tell you about Goldman and Citi." I've turned defendants over the years, but these guys were the easiest flip I've ever done.

There is a critical point here: the people at Merrill Lynch understood that their business model was problematic. They understood that there was something wrong with recommending stocks that they didn't think were any good. But they had to choose between ethics and profits, and they made the choice that harmed individuals and undercut the integrity of the market. And then they said it wasn't up to them to enforce the rules of transparency. Somebody else should do it.

Who? *Only government can do it.* The market was driving investment bankers to an unacceptable, ineffective, market-destroying standard of behavior. To protect the market, government had to come in and say something very simple: tell the truth to your customer. Tell the truth about the stock. Everyone understands that investors take risks, that analysts and investors sometimes get things wrong. The problem is intentional deception. That's what distinguishes being wrong from lying, error from fraud.

When Merrill said, "we are not as bad as our competitors," they were really saying that they needed an industry-wide solution, that if they were the only ones who had to live by some new standard, they would be at a competitive disadvantage and lose market share. That wouldn't be fair. I wasn't terribly sympathetic, but what they were saying about holding everyone to the same standard was true. So I recommended that we get everyone to agree to a common code of conduct before we'd go through the agony of making a case against the other banks.

We couldn't do it. The other banks simply didn't want to play ball until we said we had the evidence on them also. We went through the same exercise. Then we announced a global settlement. That was December 2002. I would argue that the settlement worked, but that is a separate conversation. What matters to the current conversation is that only government could get these companies to tell the truth to their customers.

Transparency is not an issue only for financial-services providers. It is important to every sector of the economy. Here's another story. We brought a case against the pharmaceutical maker GlaxoSmithKline, which was at the time marketing their drug Paxil—an antidepressant—as effective for teenagers. Paxil had been approved for other purposes, but this was off-label marketing. We found that a significant number of the clinical tests Glaxo had done proved something directly at odds with the company's claims. It was not for me as attorney general to determine whether this drug was bad or good for teenagers, but to insist on full disclosure of relevant information so that doctors and journals could make that determination.

When we sued Glaxo, they thought we wanted money. But we only wanted them to change the way they acted. We asked them to create a Web site for the clinical-testing data so that doctors and journals could make informed judgments. They agreed. The settlement became part of a longer process, a move toward substantially more disclosure when it comes to drugs and testing data.

From Glaxo's perspective, the more data they withheld, the better their profits were likely to be. They could persuade more people to use Paxil. So, again: only government can ensure integrity, transparency, and fair dealing.

And here's where I'm going to add my footnote: even though private companies compete, only government can ensure that there is competition. Everybody in business wants to be a monopolist. There's nothing wrong with wanting more market share. That's how you make money. But over the last 30 years, we lost our drive toward effective market enforcement. Free-market partisans argued that antitrust laws are unnecessary, that the market enforces itself. We can now say that is fundamentally wrong. If government doesn't enforce competition laws, then we lose the vitality and creativity that competition generates. Before AT&T was broken up in 1974, for example, you could choose between a black phone or a "princess" phone in a few colors. After the government-imposed breakup, people entered the telecom market and said, "let's do something different, something more creative, something better." The AT&T breakup did not cause all of the growth in that sector, but it is amazing how far we have come in telecom thanks to the competitive spirit it generated.

RULE 1 DOESN'T GO FAR ENOUGH—EVEN with the footnote. We still need to deal with externalities: positive or negative effects on third parties that are not factored into the price at which two private parties transact. Somebody needs to adjust for externalities that escape market-determined prices. That is the job of government, through taxes and subsidies.

Rule 2. In the face of externalities, government must intervene to change the way the market behaves.

When I was attorney general, we brought environmental cases against a bunch of Midwestern utility companies. They were burning a lot of coal, generating pollution that came down over New York. So I went down to Washington to testify about the cases. Senator George Voinovich, sitting behind the dais, looked down at me. He said, "General Spitzer, I was the governor of Ohio before I was the senator, and when I was governor we cleaned up the air in Ohio, so why are you doing this?"

I applauded him for what he did, but reminded him that one of the ways the utilities cleaned up the air in Ohio was by building smokestacks a thousand feet tall. Smokestacks that tall aren't cheap or pretty, but they do put all the carbon dioxide and sulfur dioxide up into the jet stream. It doesn't come down in

Ohio, or even Pennsylvania or New Jersey. It comes down in New York. If the pollution is coming down in New York, I told him, you're creating a negative externality in New York, and under the Clean Air Act I can sue you. And that's how to put the cost of cleaning this up back on the utilities, where it belongs.

Here's another example of an externality that most people don't think of in those terms: too much debt. The decision to incur debt seems like a perfectly private one with no spill-over effects. But when you aggregate all the debt in an economy, problems arise. Over the last decade, the United States grew so saturated with debt that the economy experienced what has become known as "systemic risk." The whole system shattered because there wasn't enough new wealth to service the debt. Individual transactions looked okay, but the aggregate effect metastasized in a way that jeopardized everyone. Thus, government has to intervene in debt markets because too much debt is a negative externality in terms of economic stability, just as excessive carbon dioxide is a negative externality in terms of global warming. In neither case can government safely stand idle.

The third area in which government has to intervene is the most elastic and, in a way, also the most important. It is what I call core values. There are certain core values—values that we as a society embrace—that the marketplace simply will not address. I'll give you two examples: ending discrimination and maintaining a minimum wage.

When I was an undergraduate, I attended a policy seminar about discrimination at Princeton's Woodrow Wilson School. One of the popular arguments we discussed is that discrimination is inefficient and that the market would therefore get rid of it: a company that would not hire men over six-feet tall would lose out on a certain universe of talent and would be less competitive. With lower profit margins, and trouble attracting capital, it eventually would go out of business. It's a very nice theory. Men over six-feet tall were not the typical group discriminated against, but it was the same argument whether it was based on gender, race, or religion.

The problem is that the theory doesn't match reality. After 200 years of market behavior, discrimination continued. It got better or worse in different eras, but the social mores that drove discrimination based on race, gender, or religion continued to overpower the rational activity of economic actors. Those mores were a more powerful motivator than the pressure to hire the best person or sell to that additional customer. We didn't begin to get rid of discrimination in this country until government passed laws that created a right of action, a way to sue for being discriminated against.

In the case of minimum wage, people ask, what is the economic argument for minimum wage? Shouldn't we let the market determine the value of labor? No. We've made a societal judgment that people who work a 40-hour week should have enough money to buy food for their kids. That's a value judgment that the market does not ensure. Government needs to intervene.

These two are merely examples of core values, and there is a large debate about what core values are—about whether they are determined politically or culturally. The term is elastic, but core values exist and define us as a community. And as long as we can understand those values, government intervention to permit and enforce them is appropriate and necessary. So we have:

Rule 3. The government needs to intervene on behalf of core values.

These three rules do not offer a universal theory that solves every problem, but they do create a rational framework that says government should be active in certain areas and for specific reasons.

COMING NOW TO THE CURRENT CRISIS: has government intervention been appropriate and effective? Perhaps not surprisingly, my conclusion is that it has not. When our economic world appeared to collapse, there was absolutely no question that an enormous sum of money was going to be spent creating solvency and liquidity; money needed to be pushed into the system. On that premise, there was universal agreement. And when it was done—the number $24 trillion is thrown about when you aggregate the straight cash given out, the guarantees, the money we printed—everyone cheered.

But when the cheering finished, three difficult questions emerged. First, who will pay the bills? Second, which regulatory reforms do you impose at the moment when you have the leverage and, in all likelihood, the only opportunity to make a change before the status quo reasserts itself? Third, how do you address the desperate need for jobs in a troubled economy?

On the first question—who pays?—a lot of people say the answer is obvious. We all do. But wait a minute: many of the executives of the companies left with enormous bonuses. There were opportunities for clawbacks, which would have required asserting claims to recover salary and bonuses paid over prior years, perhaps on a theory of unjust enrichment. In aggregate this wouldn't have been a big sum compared to all that we put in. But in terms of the message sent and the appropriateness of the remedies, this should have been considered and still could be.

The government also could have required more debt-equity swaps where the debt-holders of the companies still had claims on those companies. Forcing debt-holders to convert their debt to equity would have put them in a very different position: they would have been at risk and been held to a different standard. We could have driven the equity to zero in many of these companies that were insolvent because of their financial shenanigans, but we didn't. Think about the consequences for those who hold options in these companies, which were given a huge sum of public money, as the stock rebounds. It might have been down to two dollars, but once it hits $30, $40, $50 again—because of the huge infusion of public money—stockholders make out extremely well. Should they have been put in a position to benefit? We didn't have the discussion about whether to drive equity to zero, wiping out those option values that remained in the hands of the folks who created the mess. It is fair to ask why.

Passing the cost of the bailout straight to the taxpayer was exemplified in the case of AIG.

When AIG was being bailed out—the first investment was $85 billion—everybody said that we needed to pay off the credit default swaps (essentially insurance contracts against defaults on debt repayment). If the holders of the credit default swaps were not made whole, everything would go bad. That was rubbish. There was absolutely no reason for those counterparties to get a hundred cents on the dollar. But when Goldman showed up, and CEO Lloyd Blankfein said, "we want our $12.9 billion," Goldman, as a counterparty, got $12.9 billion.

When Larry Summers, former director of President Obama's National Economic Council, was asked why he supported the full payments to Goldman, his answer was that "we are a nation of law, where there are contracts." That's a silly answer. There was a contract, but taxpayers were not a party to it. We didn't make a deal with AIG to make whole every counterparty to every contract. Our government—

with our support—said, "let's do what needs to be done to resuscitate the economy and to make sure things don't get worse." Initially some of the low-level people at the Fed were asking the right question, trying to figure out what percentage to pay. They understood that this was the relevant question. But that question was taken off the table. The investment banks, the counterparties, got one hundred cents on the dollar, and Goldman got a check for $12.9 billion, covering most of their bonus pot. Taxpayers funded their bonuses.

But it is even worse than that. Because then the Fed and the Treasury, which were being sanctimonious about this at the time, said, "we're going to take stock in AIG." Think about it. AIG was a worthless shell. Anybody would say: "I'm giving you, as a conduit, a check for $12.9 billion; you're turning around and giving the check to Goldman? I want stock in Goldman. I don't want stock in a worthless shell." The Fed and the Treasury didn't consider that possibility. I don't know why, but it returns us to the question of who pays. The taxpayer picked up the whole bill. That was wrong.

On the second question, about regulatory reform, the government is doing even worse. Dodd-Frank is a mediocre band-aid that does not confront the critical issues of companies that are too big to fail and the now-explicit federal guarantee behind institutions that are deemed to be of systemic importance. Indeed, by recognizing that certain entities are critical cogs in the gears of the economy, the legislation institutionalizes their role and makes permanent their capacity to borrow at a lower cost than their smaller competitors.

As a result, the government is deepening its committment to the companies that are too big *not* to fail. Institutions the size of AIG underperform because they cannot be managed. The federal/taxpayer guarantee on their debt—capital at virtually zero cost—does not improve performance; it subsidizes continuing underperformance.

A global consensus has now emerged that too-big-to-fail is the biggest single threat to our bank system. Economist Henry Kaufman, a conservative voice, had a lengthy op-ed in the *Wall Street Journal* that reaches this conclusion. Paul Volcker, former Fed chairman and now chair of the President's Economic Recovery Advisory Board, agrees. Former Fed Chairman Alan Greenspan—whose autobiography is one long, standing ovation for Ayn Rand—has said that too-big-to-fail is dangerous. Mervyn King, the governor of the Bank of England, has said it. Unfortunately only two people seem not to get it: Larry Summers, recently departed from his official role in the administration, and Treasury Secretary Timothy Geithner. They say, "if it's too big to fail, we're going to backstop it." That guarantee socializes risk and privatizes gain. You do that, and you're going to get distorted investment patterns and the same excessive willingness to tolerate risk that caused all the problems in the first place.

We've also participated in a regulatory charade. All the CEOs say, "It's not our fault. The regulators didn't get it right." The regulators say, "We didn't get it right because we didn't have enough power." So everyone runs to Capitol Hill to write new laws to give regulators more power. We don't need new laws. We need regulators who will use the power they already have. Congress put in place new rules that say banks can't increase credit-card fees without getting consent from consumers. Nice idea. Why didn't they do it five years ago? All the dramatic steps the Fed has taken to resuscitate, to bail out, to restructure, to guarantee: they could have done it all before. So Congress passes a new law, there is a big signing ceremony, and everyone says it won't happen again because now the regulators have the power. They already had the power. They didn't want to use it, and passing a new law is not going to embolden them.

That's what I call the Peter Principle on Steroids. The Peter Principle, named for its originator, Dr. Laurence J. Peter, holds that people are promoted to the point of their incompetence. In the Peter Principle on Steroids, people are promoted to the point of their incompetence, but their incompetence creates a crisis, and they use the crisis to gain even more power. They get a promotion beyond the point of their incompetence because of the crisis that they created. This is what we're doing in Washington. The two entities at the heart of this crisis were the Fed and the Treasury Department. They failed. Completely, utterly failed. Now look at the reform proposals. The breakthrough idea is that the Fed is going to be our systemic-risk regulator. Wow. That's important. But I

hate to break it to you: they already are. That's
their job. That's what they were supposed to
be doing for the last twenty years.

Another bold breakthrough: the Fed's idea
to conduct "stress tests" on major banks. Great
idea. But they are banking regulators. They had
the power to do this. They just chose not to.

Think about what happened with subprime
loans. In 2004 I wrote, "These loans are foisted
on borrowers who have no realistic ability to
repay them and who face the loss of their hard-
won equity when all the inevitable defaults and
foreclosures occur."

Now I am not a banking regulator. Still,
we were trying to investigate subprime lend-
ing back in 2004 because we knew there was
a problem. I don't want anybody to misinter-
pret "foisted on" as absolving the borrower of
responsibility. Everybody bears responsibility,
and, on both sides of this transaction, people
are at fault. The point is that the consequences

to the financial sector and to the economy were clear even then.

So we tried to investigate, and the Office of the Controller of the Currency (OCC) shut us down. It went to court to block our inquiry; its partners in the courtroom were all the banks that later got TARP money. The banks that fund their bonuses with your tax dollars are the powerbrokers that stopped our 2004 inquiry into subprimes. The OCC's legal argument was "we have the power to investigate, you don't." Did the OCC investigate? No. It was too busy shutting down people who were trying to do what it should have been doing.

Regulators don't need additional power, they just need to use their existing power appropriately. And this will not happen unless different people are in charge. We are going through a huge regulatory reshuffle because what went on was absolutely horrifying. But all the laws and regulatory reforms will not matter unless we put in charge people who actually believe in enforcement.

The third question is about jobs, and here we are in deeper trouble than anyone wants to acknowledge. If you look at how many people are outside the employment structure, at what has happened to our manufacturing sector, at the few sectors that have added jobs—education and health care, which are hugely important but do not form the long-term foundation of a competitive and self-sufficient economy— the trend lines spell disaster.

It did not have to be this way. All that money we spent on bailouts could have been leveraged for job-creation. When we gave Goldman $12.9 billion and gave trillions to the banks, we didn't say, "Do something useful, do something that will create jobs." They went out and got involved in proprietary trading. If Goldman wants to make a fortune on proprietary trading, hats off to them. But they shouldn't be doing that with tax dollars and taxpayer guarantees on their investments.

Compare that $12.9 billion to the $8 billion in the stimulus package for investment in high-speed rail. More than 50 percent more went to Goldman, even though there has been consensus for years that high-speed rail is critical: for energy, for efficiency. We're not doing what needs to be done.

Or, consider the auto industry. We gave huge sums of money to resuscitate the shells of companies that probably won't come back. Here's another idea: the government could say, "We will buy 500,000 electric cars in 2013 from whoever gives us the best prototype, as long as 80 percent of production occurs domestically." It doesn't matter what the nameplate is—Kia, GM, Chrysler—but make them here. Set the number high enough so that the companies could generate a profit because of scale.

Electric cars face a major challenge, but one that also offers opportunity: you can't get very far on an interstate highway in an electric car. The government, which built the highways during the Eisenhower administration, should build recharging stations wherever there are gas stations on the interstate. That is an infrastructure project that creates jobs and eases the transition away from gasoline-powered cars and toward electric cars. We know we want to be leaders in that. We should be giving money to sectors that will invest in jobs and infrastructure in a big and fundamental way.

THE SUCCESS OF EVERYTHING I'VE DIS-cussed here depends on corporate governance. Corporations run the economy, as they should. But if we don't run our corporations properly, then we will not get ourselves out of this pit.

The chain of corporate governance includes a CEO, a board, and board committees. There are also three facilitators—lawyers, investment bankers, and accountants—who are hired to figure out how to implement the CEO's plans. Then there are shareholders, who actually own the company.

The problem lies in the abrogation of fiduciary duty, the loyalty that managers owe to owners. Fiduciary duty embodies all of corporate governance. If the decision-makers don't understand this notion—to whom they owe it and how to enforce it—nothing will work.

Let's start with an example: corporate pay. Back in the mid-'80s, the Business Roundtable—an organization of corporate America—did a study of the ratio of the average CEO's compensation to the average worker's. It was about 40:1. People said, "Okay, this is capitalism, and that's how things are." In Europe the ratio was closer to 20:1, but we believed we had a more dynamic economy, so things seemed fine. By 2000, that ratio of 40:1 had exploded to more than 500:1. No one could seriously argue that CEOs became more than ten times more valuable to companies relative to average workers. Clearly the system had broken down. Anyone who digs into the issue of corporate compensation will see that what was going on was an outrageous betrayal of fiduciary duty.

Here's another example. There's something called spinning. When an investment bank does an IPO, and the IPO is hot—the stock is going to jump on that first day of sale—they give some of these hot stocks to the CEOs of their clients. Why? To keep them happy, so they stay as clients. As attorney general I said that should not be permitted; it violates the fiduciary duty of the CEO to the company. If an investment bank wants to give away something of value to keep a company as a client, it should give its gift to the client's shareholders, not the client's CEO. There's an uglier term for spinning: commercial bribery. In 2002 we negotiated a global deal and outlawed it. People got outraged. One extremely powerful regulator today, a Peter-Principle-on-Steroids survivor, asked me then, "Don't CEOs have any rights anymore?"

These violations of fiduciary duty shape the whole system. As a result, the CEOs and compensation committees no longer focus, as they should, on company performance.

These are vexing problems, and much has been said and written about how to resuscitate corporate governance. Boards and shareholders are the only real long-run answers. Boards have to become more active, and that means they will have to be chosen in a fundamentally different way. CEOs, frankly, need to have their wings clipped because the internecine relationship between CEOs and boards has led us down a dangerous path.

Every now and then, the SEC begins to approach the problem and proposes that shareholders choose the board members. The proposal is met with indignation: shareholders, we are told, will speak like a narrow special-interest group. Well, yes, they are the owners. The opposition to the notion that shareholders actually be given power is crazy.

But the participation of shareholders is a genuinely difficult problem, in part because of the remarkable liquidity in the stock market. Owners of shares can trade and sell their positions easily. This flexibility is extremely valuable, but it also means that shareholders do not stay in for the long, hard slog of reforming companies in which they have a momentary ownership interest. Liquidity thus undermines the urgency of and the argument for participation.

Albert O. Hirschman's 1970 book, *Exit, Voice, and Loyalty*, brilliantly captures this dynamic. How do decision-makers consider the various options they face when they see a product—whether toothpaste, a political party, or a share in a company—and need to decide whether to use their voice to improve it or to exit and find something better? Hirschman presciently observed the implications of easy exit options for "perpetuating bad management": because of the "ready availability of alternative investment opportunities in the stock market . . . any resort to voice rather than to exit is unthinkable for any but the most committed stockholder." Somehow we have to overcome this problem. Perhaps shareholders should be given additional voting power if they own a stock longer. That solution has its own troubles. But we need to find a way to give shareholders the power and incentive to get involved.

Exit options are not the only hurdle to shareholder power. Consider who the largest shareholders are: mutual funds and pension funds (and university endowments, which are kind of the same thing). Why is that a problem? Lets take the case of mutual funds.

When I was attorney general, I participated in a panel on mutual funds at Harvard Law School. We were discussing whether funds should disclose their records in proxy voting, whereby a fund exercises its customers' voice on the boards of the companies it invests in. One of the participants was the general counsel for an enormous mutual fund company. She was asked whether she would disclose how her company votes its proxies. And she said no, that it would be too expensive. That was a ridiculous answer. The reason mutual fund companies don't want to tell their shareholders their votes is that mutual funds almost always vote with the management of the companies in which they hold shares. Why? Because mutual fund companies make money by increasing the size of the assets they manage, and the size of those assets is directly related to whether they are chosen by companies to be the recipient of 401(k) business. If they vote against management, they won't be put on the 401(k) option list. As a result, mutual fund companies help entrench management.

Because pension funds have never been activist either, we have denied ourselves the dynamism that we could get from the largest participants in the marketplace. CEOs and entrenched boards retain the power. We went down this path without taking a hard look at the destination.

To begin to repair corporate governance, it is important to understand what happened. I hope the Financial Crisis Inquiry Commission, which is supposedly the equivalent of the post–1929 crash Pecora Commission, will investigate information flows along two lines. The first is about how information flows up to the boards at the major banks that failed. What were they told about the creditworthiness of their positions? One possibility is that they weren't told anything, which tells us a great deal about their level of involvement. Or maybe they were told they were in a creditworthy position and need not worry. Or, they were told they were in jeopardy, but they didn't do anything. Knowing the answer would give us a better understanding of the failures of corporate management. The second line focuses on the Fed and the Treasury. What did the New York Fed, the most important regulator of banks, and the Treasury know about the debt and leverage situations of these failing banks, and what did they believe?

To sum up, I leave you with ten points:

• Only government can enforce integrity and transparency in the marketplace; self-regulation is a failure.

• Only government can take the steps necessary to overcome market failures, such as negative externalities or monopoly power.

• Only government can act to preserve certain core values in the market, such as prohibitions on discrimination.

• Too-big-to-fail is too-big-*not*-to-fail.

- We're suffering from the Peter Principle on Steroids, and it will get us into deeper trouble.
- Taxpayers have been getting the short end of the stick in everything we've been doing. The Treasury Department is not negotiating for us.
- Risk is real, and no complex scheme of financial instruments can make it go away.
- We have de-leveraged the wrong way, by socializing risks and privatizing benefits. The government has accepted all the debt obligations of the private sector, and taxpayers now owe this money.
- The only way to reform corporate governance is to get the owners—the shareholders—of companies involved and actually paying attention.
- All of this is very tough: being able to diagnose a problem is a whole lot easier than mustering the will to fix it.

II
Forum

Dean Baker

ELIOT SPITZER MAKES AN EFFECTIVE argument against much of the corruption that has taken root in our economy and society over the last three decades. However, he makes a fundamental error in portraying his agenda as a case for government intervention at odds with the free-market principles of those who have been setting economic policy. Attributing such beliefs to our economic managers is far too generous. The role of the government in the economy has changed over the last 30 years, and in some cases grown—just not in ways that protect ordinary workers and consumers.

Let's start with the most obvious example: the financial industry, or, at least, its biggest actors, which have been operating with the benefit of too-big-to-fail protection from the federal government. Banks such as J.P. Morgan and Citigroup were arguably too big to fail even three decades ago, before growth and mergers expanded their size several-fold. In the last decade these institutions grew so big that their collapse would undoubtedly have jeopardized the health of the financial system. Everyone knew that, so creditors could lend these banks money without concern for their soundness: the government, ultimately, would stand behind the debt. This has nothing to do with Ayn Rand's libertarianism. Huge financial institutions simply took advantage of taxpayers by getting insurance without having to pay for it.

Similarly, the quest for less regulatory control of banks that hold FDIC-insured deposits is not a story of deregulation. It is an effort by banks to exploit the government's insurance policy. It is comparable to running a fireworks factory out of a home where the owner pays the standard residential insurance rate. This insurance rip-off has nothing to do with the free market.

The government's involvement in the economy has grown substantially in important areas such as patent and copyright protection, but supposed proponents of free markets don't seem to mind. The percentage of GDP that is diverted to holders of patents and copyrights has risen dramatically over the last three decades as Congress has approved a number of measures that increase the length and scope of these protections. Strengthened patent and copyright protection has been felt internationally as well. Virtually every trade pact since Ronald Reagan took office has imposed more stringent patent and copyright protection on U.S. trading partners.

The impact of these measures is most visible in the case of prescription drugs. The country is projected to spend close to $274.5 billion this year, just under 2 percent of GDP, on prescription drugs. Without what amounts to government-granted patent monopolies, the cost would be close to one-tenth of this amount. Individuals and insurance companies pay the extra cost, and not just with their cash: many Americans who would have no difficulty paying the free-market price for generic drugs cannot afford to buy drugs at their patent-protected prices.

The government's role in enforcing intellectual property has led to increasing interference with the free market in other ways. The Internet has made copyrights far less enforceable, yet rather than modernizing our system for financing creative work, the government has taken extreme measures to preserve copyrights—pushing universities and high schools to promote courses on the importance of honoring copyrights; sending police into college dorms and the bedrooms of high school students in search of unauthorized copies of recorded music; and even arresting a Russian computer scientist for giving an academic lecture on methods for breaking encryption software.

This narrative that treats patents and copyrights as simply facts of nature rather than government intervention into the economy is certainly welcomed by the corporations that profit from these policies. It puts them beyond the realm of public debate. However, patent and copyrights were not given by god or nature. They are government policies for promoting innovation and creative work. Are they the best policies to accomplish these goals? It is not possible even to ask the question until we acknowledge that they are policies that can be changed.

The example of patents and copyrights is instructive because it shows how completely government policy shapes the economy. There is no free market economy, devoid of government intervention. The government sets the rules, and it can set the rules in ways that benefit the vast majority of the population, or it can set the rules in ways that have the effect of redistributing wealth and income upward, as it has over the last three decades.

Let's take another example, one that Spitzer uses: the argument that we need the government to intervene in the market in order to prevent pollution. Regulations are in place, but they are designed to protect the property of wealthy landowners. I cannot build a slaughterhouse across the street from Bill Gates's house because of zoning restrictions that prevent me from engaging in activities that reduce the value of Gates's property. How are these zoning restrictions different from restrictions on greenhouse-gas emissions or any other form of pollution? How many conservative politicians think that I should be able to erect a slaughterhouse in front of Bill Gates's home?

Progressives undermine their cause when they frame their agenda as one that imposes government constraints on the market. Market outcomes, as opposed to the dictates of government bureaucrats, have substantial appeal, especially in the United States. And the market is an incredibly valuable tool. We should be looking to restructure the market in ways that produce outcomes that are more desirable. Focusing on government intervention to override the market is both bad politics and bad policy.

Robert Johnson

Eliot Spitzer examines the role of government in markets in a clear and compelling manner. He calls for government intervention in three ways: enforcing market integrity, correcting externalities, and defending core values.

I agree that all three tasks are important, but we have to ask what it takes to have government implement them in the broad interests of society. Both left and right support enforcing market integrity over protecting specific individuals or institutions, but bringing that about in a money-drenched political system is challenging. As Mancur Olson famously pointed out in *The Logic of Collective Action*, promoting public over special interests can be massively difficult.

While an undergraduate at MIT, I learned that market economies were a means to meet social goals and that finance should serve the economy. In recent years the servant's servant became the master's master. From James Carville's 1993 comment about wanting to be reincarnated as the bond market, to the Committee to Save the World in the late 1990s (it didn't, it just set us up for a bigger bubble later), to the dawn of the present crisis, goals were defined through a lens that turned what was good for investment banks into what was good for America. An awful lot of ideological manufacturing went into this inversion between means (markets) and ends (social goals). It contorted the structure of society and, for many, made paying homage to the market a core value.

Beginning with Ronald Reagan, we have had 30 years of denigration of the role of government. Yet the god called "the market" showed that it could not be left unattended. As foreclosures of homes skyrocketed and unemployment rose to the verge of Depression levels in some areas, we found out that the wild activities over in that corner called Wall Street could spill over (externalities) and destroy the lives of hard-working people powerless to escape the damage. Faith in unfettered free markets has been shattered.

Yet the end of faith in markets has not, as in the 1930s, been replaced by faith in the public sector. The present challenge is made more difficult by the bailouts under both Bush and Obama, which unmasked Wall Street's power and influence in government and produced outcomes most Americans considered offensive and unjust. Our government lost legitimacy before our eyes. The dreadful bailouts reinforced the Reagan mantra that "government is not the solution to our problem; government is the problem."

Not only have we lost faith in markets and government, but expertise is now widely suspect as well. Who can be a trusted expert? After all, most noteworthy financiers, corporate leaders, economists, and finance professors went along with bubble finance without registering any concern. All the mathematical and statistical models that economists and financial specialists developed don't matter for much if they could not predict the crisis, explain it *ex post*, or provide useful remedies. Many social scientists and financial regulators were enablers or, at best, hid while Wall Street spun out of control.

Without trust in markets, government, or experts, what is the path forward?

We must first accept that drawing simple distinctions between markets and government as means to social ends may not be realistic. Economics Nobel laureate George Stigler's 1971 critique of government and regulatory policy as susceptible to capture is even more germane in the era of wide-open corporate campaign finance, turbocharged by last year's Supreme Court decision in *Citizens United vs. Federal Election Commission. Citizens United* makes it even more difficult to keep government focused on market integrity and correcting externalities. The too-big-to-fail banks have spent upwards of $300 million on lobbying and campaign contributions to preserve the $7–10 billion (20–30 percent of their earnings) they might lose with proper reforms of derivatives markets. Unfortunately, they have succeeded in protecting those earnings and left taxpayers

bearing heightened risk that Wall Street reck-
lessness will spill over onto them, forcing them
to pay for another bailout.

We know what financial reforms are necessary; we just cannot expect the government
to make them. That is why Spitzer's discussion of core values, to my mind, suggests the
path forward.

People were angry when the government
used their tax dollars to funnel money through
AIG to Wall Street and bail out Goldman Sachs
and foreign banks. The taxpayer was left with
worthless shares of AIG when it should have
held stock in Goldman and the foreign banks
that were given a windfall. The discrepancy
between a just outcome and the one we experienced engendered rage. Our core values
were trampled.

Policymakers whine that they had to put
out the fire, but everyone knew that they did
not have to put it out precisely that way. And

even if the bailout had to be structured the way it was, the unfairness of the outcome should have made policymakers run to Congress to enact emergency reforms on behalf of the American people. Society neither can nor should tolerate what happened with AIG: it was crony capitalism in raw form.

We cannot develop trust in any pillar of our society unless we openly express and credibly foster outcomes that are consistent with our core values. We must measure ethical outcomes, not theories of potential outcomes.

How do we do this? We might start by altering the incentives that elected officials face. We have to free them from the chains of fundraising so that they can enact good policy without committing electoral suicide. At the same time, we must demand that they give up the money blanket that incumbent insurance provides. Challengers cannot sell policy, only elected officials can.

At present I sense no urgency to make such changes. But the pressure can come when people start insisting that markets dominated by large, ungovernable firms, with government acting as their toadies, violate the essence of what the country stands for. Perhaps then we will be able to rebuild the true potential of government to correct externalities, enhance market integrity, and enforce the values we all hold dear.

III

Common Sense

DEAN BAKER PROPERLY CALLS THE LIB-
ertarian ideology of the past 30 years a mere
façade behind which government actively
participated in the crafting of rules and
priorities that benefited specific groups—
banks, big pharma, certain land owners. I
surely do not believe that more than a few
intellectuals of the right actually subscribed
to the theory that a market could exist with-

out government and rules-enforcement. Virtually all who mouthed libertarian rhetoric fully understood that the battle was over whose interests would be protected and how the fruits of the economy would be distributed.

Having said that, the total embrace of the language of libertarianism in public discourse has created a deep public ambivalence, even disdain, for government over the years. While the public discussion from the 1940s through the 1970s recognized the potential of an active government, that very premise has since been rejected. Consequently, we need to rebuild the intellectual foundation that supports positive views of government participation. Having both theory and stories to do so is a critical part of successful persuasion.

Even if the public is persuaded, how can we obtain results in Congress? Political scientists John Sides, Sarah Binder, and Andrew Gelman pointed out in the March/April 2009 issue of

Boston Review that even when the public over-whelmingly favors specific legislative measures, it almost never punishes those legislators who fail to enact them. Part of the problem is that public support is often broad-based and diffuse—especially so in the case of financial reform—while opposition is narrow but deep and well funded.

This superiority of the well organized and well funded is in the blood of Washington politics. Special interests outmaneuver the public, which is too disorganized to bring focused pressure to bear on legislators. This has stymied major reform efforts across all substantive areas for several decades now. If we cannot resolve this problem, we may continue to wander aimlessly in the wilderness as the rest of the world leapfrogs over us. The theoretical reasons behind our immobilization are well explained by Mancur Olson in *The Rise and Decline of Nations* and by Albert Hirschman in *Exit, Voice, and Loyalty*.

Robert Johnson's own market acumen and wizardry give special import to his ongoing critique of the Obama administration's rather thin efforts at reform. Johnson's testimony on derivatives regulation and the risk we face if we fail to do more than has so far been achieved makes clear that toxins are still seeping into our financial system. The continuing ability of the largest market players in derivatives to rewrite reform proposals speaks to the political dynamic that Sides, Binder, and Gelman rightly identified as the source of frustration.

Johnson directs our attention to the issue most critical to a better future: our core values. Oddly, that area of public debate has been largely neglected. We have had too much chatter about mechanics and not enough about objectives—too much debate about credit default swaps and not enough about basic decency, common sense, and which outcomes the market is supposed to produce.

I strongly believe we need to start a discussion that challenges those of us who support a more active role for government to define what parameters should shape that role and why it is so important that they do. We have to undo decades of anti-government rhetoric that has metastasized into cynicism and the belief that government cannot accomplish anything useful. It is precisely that cynicism that the likes of Frank Luntz have been calling upon Republicans to harness in opposition to the sorts of reforms that many of us think are critical. We have failed to respond in kind. The progressives' task, then, demands both intellectual creativity and communication skills. The wave of populist sentiment now coursing through the country has largely been captured by the unthinking "solutions" of Sarah Palin and Glenn Beck, which makes our work so much more important. But much rides on the outcome.

ABOUT THE CONTRIBUTORS

ELIOT SPITZER is former Governor and Attorney General of New York and cohost of *Parker Spitzer* on CNN.

DEAN BAKER is Co-Director of the Center for Economic and Policy Research and author of *Taking Economics Seriously* and *False Profits*.

ROBERT JOHNSON is Director of the Project on Global Finance at the Roosevelt Institute.

BOSTON REVIEW BOOKS

Boston Review Books is an imprint of *Boston Review*, a bi-monthly magazine of ideas. The book series, like the magazine, is animated by hope, committed to equality, and convinced that the imagination eludes political categories. Visit bostonreview.net for more information.

The End of the Wild   STEPHEN M. MEYER

God and the Welfare State   LEW DALY

Making Aid Work   ABHIJIT VINAYAK BANERJEE

The Story of Cruel and Unusual   COLIN DAYAN

What We Know About Climate Change   KERRY EMANUEL

Movies and the Moral Adventure of Life   ALAN A. STONE

The Road to Democracy in Iran   AKBAR GANJI

Why Nuclear Disarmament Matters   HANS BLIX

Race, Incarceration, and American Values   GLENN C. LOURY

The Men in My Life   VIVIAN GORNICK

Africa's Turn?   EDWARD MIGUEL

Inventing American History   WILLIAM HOGELAND

After America's Midlife Crisis   MICHAEL GECAN

Why We Cooperate   MICHAEL TOMASELLO

Taking Economics Seriously   DEAN BAKER

Rule of Law, Misrule of Men   ELAINE SCARRY

Immigrants and the Right to Stay   JOSEPH H. CARENS

Preparing for Climate Change   MICHAEL D. MASTRANDREA
                               & STEPHEN H. SCHNEIDER